Symbols, Landmarks, and Monuments

The
United States
Supreme Court

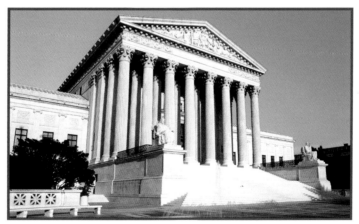

Tamara L. Britton
ABDO Publishing Company

visit us at
www.abdopub.com

Published by ABDO Publishing Company, 4940 Viking Drive, Edina, Minnesota 55435.
Copyright © 2004 by Abdo Consulting Group, Inc. International copyrights reserved in
all countries. No part of this book may be reproduced in any form without written
permission from the publisher.

Printed in the United States.

Cover Photo: Corbis
Interior Photos: Corbis pp. 1, 5, 6-7, 9, 11, 12, 13, 19, 21, 22, 24, 25, 26, 27, 28;
    Getty Images pp. 14, 15, 17, 18, 29; National Park Service p. 23

Series Coordinator: Kristin Van Cleaf
Editors: Kate A. Conley, Stephanie Hedlund
Art Direction & Maps: Neil Klinepier

Library of Congress Cataloging-in-Publication Data

Britton, Tamara L., 1963-
    The United States Supreme Court / Tamara L. Britton.
        p. cm. -- (Symbols, landmarks, and monuments)
    Includes index.
    Summary: An overview of the history, structure, and function of the United States
Supreme Court.
    ISBN 1-59197-522-0
    1. United States. Supreme Court--Juvenile literature. 2. Courts of last resort--
United States--Juvenile literature. [1. United States. Supreme Court.] I. Title.

KF8742.Z9B75 2004
347.73'26--dc22

                                                              2003062772

Contents

The Supreme Court

The **Founding Fathers** created the United States government with a system of checks and balances. The system allows the three branches of government to have power over each other. This way, one person or group cannot have all of the nation's political power.

A main part of this system is the United States Supreme Court. It is the head of the judicial branch, and the nation's most powerful court. It can declare any local, state, or federal law invalid.

The Supreme Court meets in Washington, D.C. Today, the Court's role is heavily **debated**. However, most Americans agree the Court is an important part of the U.S. system of government. It is a symbol of American **democracy**.

The Supreme Court Building

Fast Facts

√ Around 7,500 cases are sent to the Supreme Court every year. Out of these, only 80 to 100 are actually heard by the Court.

√ Congress allowed $9,740,000 to be spent on the Supreme Court Building, but it wasn't all used. In the end, $94,000 was returned to the treasury.

√ One of the building's statues is of its designer, Cass Gilbert. Another is of Robert Aitken, the artist who created the sculptures.

√ Each of the bronze doors at the front of the Supreme Court Building weighs almost seven tons (6 t)!

√ The Supreme Court's third-floor library holds more than 450,000 books.

√ Justices are often former senators or representatives. One president, William Howard Taft, later became a justice.

√ At 32 years old, Joseph Story was the youngest person to become a justice. At age 65, Horace Lurton was the oldest.

√ William O. Douglas served the longest term of any justice at 36 years, 6 months, and 25 days.

Timeline

<u>1775-1783</u>	√	Revolutionary War
<u>1787</u>	√	The Founding Fathers wrote a new constitution with three government branches and a system for balance of power.
<u>1789</u>	√	The Judiciary Act created the Supreme Court.
<u>1790</u>	√	On February 2, the Supreme Court met for the first time in the New York Merchants Exchange Building.
<u>1790-1800</u>	√	The Court met in the Philadelphia State House, and later city hall.
<u>1792</u>	√	The Supreme Court handed down its first decision.
<u>1800</u>	√	The Court moved with the federal government to Washington, D.C., where it met in the Capitol Building.
<u>1929</u>	√	Congress authorized a Supreme Court Building.
<u>1932</u>	√	Construction of the building began.
<u>1935</u>	√	The Supreme Court moved into its own building.
<u>1967</u>	√	The first African-American justice joined the Court.
<u>1981</u>	√	The first female justice was sworn in.
<u>2003</u>	√	A project began to modernize the Supreme Court Building.

A New Government

The United States began as 13 British colonies. The colonies were ruled by England's king George III and **Parliament**. Together, they held absolute power. So, the government could not be challenged, even when citizens felt laws were unfair. In 1775, this led to the **Revolutionary War**.

Eight years later, the United States was an independent nation. In 1787, the **Founding Fathers** wrote the new country's **constitution**. They decided to create a government in which power was shared.

The Founding Fathers did this by dividing the government into executive, legislative, and judicial branches. They called this separation of power. In this system, the president holds executive power. Congress has legislative power, and the Supreme Court holds judicial power.

The Founding Fathers discuss a new government.

The **Founding Fathers** weren't sure if separation of power would be enough to guard against the misuse of authority. So, they created a system called checks and balances. The system gives each branch a role in the actions of the other branches.

For example, in this system the president has power over the Supreme Court by appointing justices. Congress can also pass **constitutional amendments** to overrule the Court's decisions. But, the Court can declare presidential actions or laws passed by Congress **unconstitutional**.

The U.S. Constitution lays out the framework of the three government branches. The Supreme Court is mentioned in Article III, Section 1. It states that "The judicial Power of the United States, shall be vested in one supreme Court . . ."

The Court was officially created when the Judiciary Act of 1789 was signed into law. The United States Supreme Court met for the first time on February 2, 1790. It handed down its first decision in 1792.

The U.S. Federal Court System

All Cases End Here

The State Courts

Each state has its own court system with its own names and methods. Cases about local laws usually start in either the local or the county trial courts. They may move up through the appeals courts and end at the state's court of last resort. If a case has to do with a federal law, it may move on to the U.S. Supreme Court.

United States Supreme Court

Appellate Courts
- **U.S. Court of Appeals**
- **U.S. Court of Military Appeals**

Special Federal Courts
- **Military Courts**
- **Court of Veterans Appeals**
- **Tax Court**

Federal Trial Courts
- **U.S. District Courts**
- **Federal Claims Court**
- **U.S. Court of International Trade**

All Federal Cases Start Here

The Court's Duties

The U.S. **Constitution** is the highest law of the United States. The Supreme Court's main function is to decide whether laws follow the Constitution. Court decisions are final. They can only be changed by a constitutional **amendment** or a decision of a later Supreme Court.

The Court can declare any law invalid if a majority of the justices feels it disagrees with the Constitution. This power is called judicial review. Justices have canceled more than 1,000 laws using judicial review.

The Constitution states that the Supreme Court should hear cases affecting foreign diplomats. It should also hear cases between states, or those

Cameras have never been allowed in Supreme Court chambers. Instead, artists sketch scenes, such as this one from the 1800s.

of the federal government against a state. These types of cases make up the Court's original **jurisdiction**. They go directly to the Supreme Court.

The Court also has appellate jurisdiction. This means it can hear an appeal of a lower court's decision. Most often, a **writ of certiorari** sends the appeal to the Supreme Court. Four justices must agree to hear a case before a writ is granted.

People of the Court

The justices are the center of the Supreme Court.
Congress decides how many the Court should have. In 1869,
Congress decided the Court would have nine justices. One is
the chief justice, and the other eight are associate justices.
Since then, the number of justices has not changed.

Associate Justice Clarence Thomas (right) *stands in his office with his clerks.*

The president appoints the justices. The appointees must be confirmed by a majority of the Senate. Once confirmed, justices serve for life. They can only be removed by **impeachment** for serious wrongdoing. On average, justices serve about 15 years before retiring.

The justices are supported by aides, clerks, librarians, marshals, secretaries, and many others. The clerk manages the Court's judicial business. The marshal manages how the Court operates. The marshal and the clerk each has a staff to help him or her.

Attorneys are another important part of the Court. They must be approved before they are allowed to argue in front of it. The U.S. solicitor general is the attorney who represents the federal government during a trial.

Associate Justice Sandra Day O'Connor (center) *poses with her staff.*

How the Court Works

The Court begins for the year on the first Monday in October. It has seven two-week sittings. Each sitting is followed by a two-week recess. During sittings, the justices hear cases and deliver decisions. During recesses, the justices attend to Court business.

Justices hear **testimony** Monday through Wednesday. They take the bench at 10:00 AM. The justices have written summaries and briefs about each case. The plaintiff and the defendant each has 30 minutes to present a summary. During this time, justices ask questions about the case.

On Thursdays, the justices research cases, write **opinions**, and attend to other business. They meet on Fridays to discuss the cases they have heard. After their discussion, the justices vote. The most junior associate justice votes first, and the chief justice votes last.

The Court Chamber is where the justices hear cases.

There is an odd number of justices, so if a vote is not **unanimous** it will have a majority and a minority. For example, the vote may result in five justices voting yes and four voting no. The five justices who voted yes are the majority.

If the chief justice is in the majority, he or she chooses who will write the majority **opinion**. Otherwise, the majority's most senior justice will choose who writes it.

Justice Sandra Day O'Connor

Sandra Day O'Connor was the first woman ever appointed to the U.S. Supreme Court. She was born in 1930 and grew up in El Paso, Texas. She earned a degree in law at Stanford University in 1952. For a time, O'Connor lived in West Germany with her husband, working as a lawyer for the U.S. Army. She later moved to Arizona and became a senator. In 1981, President Ronald Reagan appointed her as a Supreme Court associate justice.

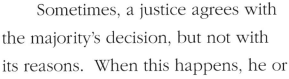

Sometimes, a justice agrees with the majority's decision, but not with its reasons. When this happens, he or she may write a **concurring opinion**. Justices in the minority may write a **dissenting** opinion if they wish.

The Court breaks in late June. During the summer, the justices are still hard at work. They decide which new cases to hear. And, they prepare for cases they will hear in the fall.

Where Is It?

The Supreme Court Building is in Washington, D.C. It stands near the U.S. Capitol Building. But the Court did not always have its own place to meet. The journey to its own building was a long one.

When the United States was a young nation, its capital changed many times. New York City was its first capital. When the Supreme Court first began, the justices met in the New York Merchants Exchange Building.

In 1790, the nation's capital moved to Philadelphia, Pennsylvania. At that time, the Supreme Court met in the State House, which became Independence Hall. Later, the Court met in the city hall.

In 1800, the nation's capital settled at its permanent home in Washington, D.C. But, the Supreme Court still did not have its own building. Congress let the Court meet in the Capitol. But, it often had to change rooms there.

In 1929, Congress authorized the building of the Supreme Court Building. A site was chosen east of the Capitol. Construction began in 1932, and the Court moved into the new building in 1935.

A hall in the Supreme Court Building shortly after the building was finished

The building's entrance is on the west side, facing the Capitol. Statues are on the east and west ends of the marble building. Stairs lead up to the entrance. At the top of the steps are 16 marble columns. Carved above them are the words "Equal Justice Under Law."

Heavy bronze doors open into the Great Hall. The hall leads into the Court Chamber. This is where the Court hears cases. The rest of the building contains a library, dining room, conference room, and offices for the justices and other Court employees.

This statue, called Guardian *or* Authority of Law, *sits to the right of the building's main stairs.*

In 2003, the Court began a project to modernize the building. Its five floors will be renovated. In addition, a Court police station will be built underground next to the building. The project should finish in 2008.

The Supreme Court Building in Washington, D.C.

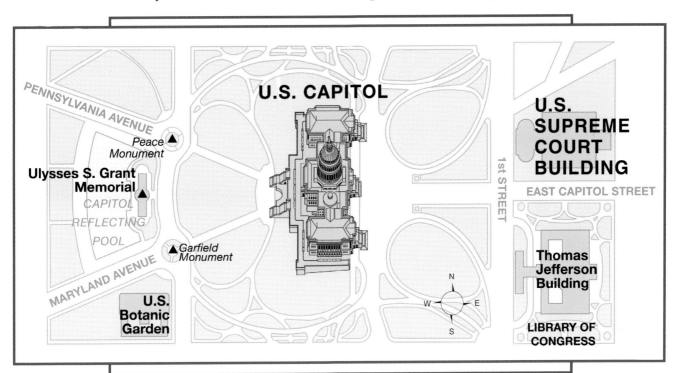

Famous Cases

Over the years, the Supreme Court has handed down a number of important decisions. As times change, so do the attitudes of the justices. As a result, some of these decisions have changed American society.

In 1803, the Court heard a case called *Marbury v. Madison.* The decision said that the Supreme Court could declare acts of Congress **unconstitutional**. This reinforced the power of judicial review.

Another well-known case is *Scott v. Sanford,* also known as the Dred Scott Decision. In 1857, the Court ruled that African-American people were not citizens of the United States. This meant they could not use the nation's court system. It limited the rights of all African Americans.

A newspaper article on the Dred Scott Decision shows illustrations of Dred Scott and his family.

Then in 1896, the Court ruled in favor of **segregation**. The *Plessy v. Ferguson* decision said that separate schools for African-American and white children were acceptable. But, the schools must offer equal services. The policy was called separate but equal.

Plessy v. Ferguson *said that separate drinking fountains for African Americans were legal.*

FOR COLORED ONLY

However in 1954, a later Court reversed this decision in *Brown v. Board of Education of Topeka.* In this case, the justices ruled that separate could not be equal. The decision said that public schools must be integrated. It suggested that racial **segregation** was no longer legal.

Sometimes, the Court's decisions reinforce people's rights. The 1963 case *Gideon v. Wainwright* decided that states should provide a lawyer to those who could not afford one. In 1966, *Miranda v. Arizona* ruled that people in police custody must be informed of their rights.

A more recent case was *Bush v. Gore.* This case decided who would win the 2000 presidential election. In a five to four vote, the Court ruled the state of Florida should not continue to recount votes. This resulted in George W. Bush becoming president.

Justice Thurgood Marshall

Thurgood Marshall was the first African-American justice to serve on the U.S. Supreme Court. Marshall was born in 1908 in Maryland and eventually studied at Howard University Law School in Washington, D.C. Marshall went on to work as a lawyer for the National Association for the Advancement of Colored People. He successfully argued to end school segregation in *Brown v. Board of Education of Topeka*. In 1967, President Lyndon B. Johnson appointed him to the Supreme Court. Marshall continued to fight for equality for all Americans before retiring in 1991. He died in 1993.

Thurgood Marshall

The Court Today

The Supreme Court's role is often **debated**. Some people believe the Court has too much power. They feel that because it can decide whether laws are **unconstitutional**, it is making laws. However, making laws is the responsibility of Congress, not of the Supreme Court.

Americans protest in front of the Supreme Court Building during the 2000 election.

Some Americans also debate how the Court should interpret the **Constitution**. Some believe it should be a "living" document. This means it is interpreted in the spirit of the times. But others believe the justices should try to decide what the **Founding Fathers** intended when they wrote the Constitution.

Americans enjoy the right to question their government. Sometimes, they disagree with the Supreme Court's decisions. But many understand that it plays an important role in defending their rights. They know it assures the United States's **democratic** system of government.

A protester waves an American flag in front of the Supreme Court Building.

Glossary

amendment - a change to a country's constitution.

concur - to act together, to agree.

Constitution - the laws that govern the United States.

debate - to discuss a question or topic, often publicly.

democracy - a governmental system in which the people vote on how to run their country.

dissent - to have a different opinion.

Founding Fathers - the men who helped write the U.S. Constitution.

impeach - to charge a public official with misconduct in office.

jurisdiction - an area where a particular group has power to govern or enforce laws.

opinion - a written explanation of the Court or majority's decision.

Parliament - England's highest lawmaking body.

Revolutionary War - from 1775 to 1783. A war for independence between Britain and its North American colonies. The colonists won and created the United States of America.

segregation - the separation of an individual or group from a larger group.

testimony - a statement given by someone under oath to tell the truth.

unanimous - when everyone in a group agrees.

unconstitutional - when a law or action goes against the Constitution.

writ of certiorari - a written order telling a lower court to send a case's records to the Supreme Court for review.

Web Sites

To learn more about the Supreme Court, visit ABDO Publishing Company on the World Wide Web at **www.abdopub.com**. Web sites about the high Court are featured on our Book Links page. These links are routinely monitored and updated to provide the most current information available.

Index